The Champion Mindset

ADVANCE PRAISE

One of the most VALUABLE reads in the marketplace on the Law of Attraction. Ginny Gane did a phenomenal job of explaining those "missing pieces" that so many have lacked in their explanations over the years of how to apply the LOA in your everyday life. I will put this read right up there with the golden "crew" of Jim Rohn and Esther Hicks in the personal development and LOA realm. Amazing. – *Angie E.*

Freaking awesome! Chapter six is my favorite... "you don't have to figure it out" was one of the big ah-ha moments for me when I started to realize this! THANK YOU – *Nick A.*

Before reading this book, all I knew about the Law of Attraction was "like attracts like." I didn't know the scientific reasons behind it -- and yes there are some! The author does a great job of explaining in a way that is concrete, not just "woo-woo." This helped me accept LOA as an actual "law", like the laws of math or physics. I particularly love her chapter about gratitude and appreciation. I read this book on a flight to a conference. When I read this chapter, I stopped a moment to appreciate a few things in my life... when I landed and got to my hotel, I found out they had upgraded me to the Presidential Suite! I don't know if my appreciation directly manifested a massive hotel suite, but I couldn't help but *appreciate* what happened! – *Tami S.*

The Champion Mindset is a definite must have for anyone who is interested in learning to use the Law of Attraction to help create the life they want. It is an easy and concise read. Ginny explains the concepts of Law of Attraction in simple language that make sense to someone brand new to the learning about the power of deliberate creation, and at the same time also very beneficial to those who have known about the law for years. I am so grateful to have this book as part of my library now so that I can refer to it over and over. I can't recommend *The Champion Mindset* highly enough! – *Anne Marie R.*

THE
CHAMPION
MINDSET

ACCESS YOUR POWER TO CREATE
LEVERAGING THE LAW OF ATTRACTION

BY
GINNY GANE

NEW YORK

NASHVILLE • MELBOURNE • VANCOUVER

THE CHAMPION MINDSET

Access Your Power to Create Leveraging the Law of Attraction

Published in New York, New York, by Morgan James Publishing in partnership with Difference Press. Morgan James is a trademark of Morgan James, LLC.
www.MorganJamesPublishing.com

The Morgan James Speakers Group can bring authors to your live event. For more information or to book an event visit The Morgan James Speakers Group at www.TheMorganJamesSpeakersGroup.com.

ISBN 9781683503859 paperback
ISBN 9781683503866 eBook
Library of Congress Control Number: 2016920213

Cover Design by:
Megan Whitney
megan@creativeninjadesigns.com

Interior Design by:
Chris Treccani
www.3dogdesign.net

In an effort to support local communities, raise awareness and funds, Morgan James Publishing donates a percentage of all book sales for the life of each book to Habitat for Humanity Peninsula and Greater Williamsburg.

Get involved today! Visit
www.MorganJamesBuilds.com

TABLE OF CONTENTS

INTRODUCTION

Seven hundred years ago if someone walked up to you and told you the earth was round, you would laugh in their face because you obviously knew the earth was flat. If 200 years ago, an individual mentioned the idea of one day being able to talk to a person on the other side of the world or that we would fly in planes across oceans or be able to create human organs, you would again laugh in their face because your mind at that time could not conceive of that being a reality. And yet, those things are our reality now. Isn't that interesting to consider? What we know to be reality is not permanent, but constantly expanding and changing. Our reality and what we believe is possible... is dynamic.

So now when I tell you (read this next part slowly) that you CAN be, do or have ANYTHING you desire, how does that make you feel? Maybe you feel a shy excitement at the thought as a smile comes across your face, or potentially you feel doubtful at the idea.

When I started working with my client Jesse, he had already known about the Law of Attraction for a few years and really believed in everything he heard and read, but hadn't really noticed any changes in his life because of it. He was talking about stresses at work, and when I asked, well what do you want your work experience to be like, after a couple moments thinking about it, he kind of exploded with "I want to love what I do, I want my superiors to trust and appreciate me, I want more freedom, I want to work from home." He admitted that he hadn't really thought about what he wanted as much as he thought about what was the normal experience for most people, and what society taught him was generally conceivable.

Who determines what is real and possible? Who sets the boundaries for who you can be and what you can do? Have you ever considered that this life is all about you and what you want? You are the one who gets to create your own life.

You hold all the power to be and experience everything you desire.

There is no limit and throughout this book, I am going to show you the potential you have to deliberately manifest your desires. If you want to meet the love of your life, live in your dream home, build a business you love or simply fall in love with your life, you CAN! Your power as a creator is limited only by your own imagination.

I work with clients to help them get unstuck and move forward on their path. They come to me because they are looking for clarity, success and relief from the struggle and I teach them the principles and skills of the Law of Attraction and how it plays out in their lives. I'm writing this book because after I completed post secondary education, I was still lost. I didn't know what I wanted in my life and was searching for how I could really get everything I want and reach my potential as an individual. From the moment I read my first Abraham-Hicks book, everything clicked. I effortlessly started applying the principles and life became fun, exciting and so much easier! My path became clear and I began experiencing the joy of this life on a whole new level. Presently Jesse works at his new job from home, totally free and reporting to me by email that "I have an Awesome job, and the people I work with are so cool!" - And so, my hope is to help you experience the same clarity, joy and ease as I and so many of my clients have. In this book I'm going to walk you through certain principles of the Law of Attraction that will lead you to a life you love.

There is nothing that you want, that you cannot have. It is my belief that we are here on this planet to ultimately experience the joy of existence. We are not here to acquire the stuff: cars, toys, houses, jobs. We are here for growth, expansion and joy. The manifestations are simply by-products of us finding connection with our true selves and stepping into the person we want to be. It is along the path to your manifestations that life happens and you become all that you can be.

You are Your Own Teacher

During the next few hours of your life, depending on how fast you read, you are going to learn about the universal law of attraction, how you can become a master at leveraging this invisible force and understanding your own potential to create and live the life you dream about. This book will reinforce how, you, exactly where you are, exactly who you are, with your job, partner, haircut, body, have the absolute power to create the life that you dream of. It is so possible and real, and all of those things that you imagine and daydream about can become your reality. Although I do not believe that words alone can cause full transformation, I believe that words have the potential to inspire vibrational shifts. Words carry energy and I know without a doubt that you can have it all. It is my desire that as I share my vibrational interpretations and from my vibrational perspective, it will help guide you to your own understanding and knowing of who you really are. This is going to be such a fun adventure in co-creation!

CHAPTER 1.

LOA Works and Here's Why

———————————

When I first started working last year with Simon, he wanted to feel the joy in this life that so many people claim to feel. He had recently learned about the Law of Attraction and was doing his best to think positive but he wasn't feeling any different. Simon wasn't bringing more joy into his life because he didn't yet understand, not only how the law of attraction works, but also why. To really be able to consciously create a life you love, first you need to be aware how and why the

Law of Attraction works and the principles. And that's what I teach you in this chapter.

WE LIVE IN A VIBRATIONAL UNIVERSE

It was so fascinating the first time I learned about vibration, frequency, atoms and electrons. And when a wise teacher informed me that when we take it down to a sub-atomic level, we do not find matter but only pure energy, I was like wait...what? You're telling me that everything in this whole world is made up of the same thing? And it is energy? (This totally blew my mind) Yes, science shows us that at the core of human bodies and all matter on this physical earth is energy. The same energy that composes the human body is the same as the solid forms we see like trees or cars or houses. The only difference is that the energy is vibrating at different vibrational frequencies. Every thing (car, tree, table) has its own vibrational frequency, and we translate these different frequencies to represent various forms. Because the Law of Attraction is grounded in the interaction of vibrations, you can now grasp how essential it is to understand that we live in a vibrational universe.

WE ARE ALL CONNECTED

The English mathematician Paul Dirac first postulated that there is no such thing as nothingness, or empty space. It may appear to you that you are separate from other people and other things, like the car or table, but in actuality we are all connected at the most basic level of energy. Researchers have proved mathematically that everywhere, even inside our own bodies, atoms and molecules are engaged in an instantaneous and ceaseless passing back and forth of information. We are constantly communicating and interacting with the energy around us similar to tiny balls of vibrating waves passing energy back and forth like an endless game of basketball. Ultimately we are a small but vital part of this one energy, this big ball of ever-dynamic vibration, we call the universe.

You are a ghost, driving a meat-coated skeleton, made of stardust, riding a rock, floating through space. Fear Nothing. – **Anonymous**

Our universe is actually governed by a set of laws. The same as we have traffic laws in order to produce ease and harmony when driving on roads, we have universal laws that allow perfect harmony with our existence in this universe. Stated by Albert Einstein, "We live in an orderly universe. There are universal laws that govern the process of Nature that extend throughout infinity." These laws, based in The Akashic Records, and now grounded in physics and solid scientific evidence, originate as far back as five thousand years ago. The Law of Attraction has its foundation in and runs through all of the primary laws, holding everything together.

We are in every moment emitting a vibration out to the surrounding universal vibrations, and the universe is responding back to us.

Now you know what I mean when I say everything is energy. Everything in this universe vibrates and is in constant vibratory motion. This is the reason we are able to influence our reality. We are composed of the same energy as that of everything around us, and there is a constant interaction between the energies.

We are in every moment emitting a vibration out to the surrounding universal vibrations, and the universe is responding back to us.

The Danish physicist Niels Bohr discovered that once sub-atomic particles such as electrons or photons are in contact, they remain cognizant of and influenced by each other instantaneously over any distance forever. This describes what scientists have termed "Quantum Entanglement." In other words, sub-atomic particles or vibration, which are the basis of all matter and non-matter, have the potential to be influenced by other vibrations.

WE COMMUNICATE THROUGH EMOTIONS

It is our emotions that act as the vehicle in translating vibration. Our emotions are what allow us the power to communicate with the universe. Each emotion that you feel carries with it a different vibrational frequency. Therefore the emotion that you are feeling determines what you are putting out and communicating with the universe. It is our emotions that are our universal language.

The universe doesn't hear spoken words or language it is the vibration or the feeling behind the words that is most important.

I'm sure you can think of a time when you have said something, but didn't really mean it. Maybe you have been wanting to take a vacation to Italy for years and your friend calls you up to say she just booked her flight to Tuscany for three weeks, you say "Oh, that's great, I am so excited for you!" But... are you really happy for her? Or is it more of a "I'm happy for you, but I wish it was me" kind of deal. Because there is a difference! The universe is going to hear and respond to your feeling emotion, not your words.

The universe doesn't hear spoken words or language it is the vibration or the feeling behind the words that is most important.

You can think of your emotions as being like radio stations that you dial into to listen in your car or on your boom box. Boom boxes are still a thing right? You turn the dial to 88.5 and are tuned into that station, receiving and listening to the music of that station. Fun and joy correspond to 88.5, so you tune into that frequency to feel those emotions, and in chapter four, you are going to learn all about how you can easily tune in to what you want!

THE EMOTIONAL CONNECTION

Like the stations move up from 88.1 to 107.9 on the radio frequency scale, we also have an emotional guidance scale ranging from fear at the lowest to love at the highest. Each emotion corresponds to a specific vibrational frequency, and when you are feeling a specific emotion, it is that frequency of vibration you are emitting to the universe. For example, you are stuck in traffic and become frustrated because you are late to your appointment. The feeling of frustration emits a certain frequency out to the universe, and the Law of Attraction responds by bringing you things in your reality that match the frustration vibration, maybe you spill your coffee or remember you forgot to put the wash in.

This illustrates how what you feel about something or someone is being sent out like information waves and being received by the broader non-physical energy. It is interesting to observe how much we communicate with each other through vibration as well. Have you ever met someone and can immediately get a "feel" for them? Generally you know if someone is having a good or bad day as soon as you get close to them or speak with them, because you can intuitively feel it. There is an associated vibration with everything.

Brain science research has shown us that emotional responses create physical changes in our bodies. When fear is physically experienced, it activates a collection of nerve cells in the brain called the amygdala. Interestingly here though, is that even if you show happy people fearful faces, the amygdala activates as if those people were experiencing the fear themselves. Even more intriguing, when you make those same people unaware that they are seeing fearful faces, the brain response in the amygdala is the same. Their brain is responding to the fear emotion. Therefore fear in others will register in our brains as our own fear. We are connected to other people and their brains through vibration. This makes sense why when you are around an anxious person, you start to feel anxious or the opposite happens as well; if you are surrounded by happy positive people it is easier to feel good.

THE LAW OF ATTRACTION

The Law of Attraction simply states like attracts like. Because we live in this vibrational universe, where everything is energy, it can be explained further by saying similar vibrations are naturally drawn or attracted to each other. You can also think of it like two of the same vibrations being magnetized or pulled together.

Have you ever observed how you naturally gravitate towards people that share the same interests as you? If you are someone who values health and fitness, likely a good portion of your close people also take an interest in this. Birds of the same feather, flock together, is actually saying like attracts like. As you become aware of your vibrational reality, you begin to understand why you are experiencing certain people, things or events in your life.

Having this awareness is the first step on your path to being the conscious deliberate creator of your life, and understanding the Law of Attraction will allow you to align with the greater divine universal energy and achieve the mastery of this life you are looking for. During my second session with Andrea, a client working on manifesting a new lover, she made the comment "Oh I always date the bad boys..." Shortly followed by an "ohhhh, I didn't realize I thought that, no wonder I keep dating the same kind of guy!"

LAW OF ATTRACTION PRINCIPLES

The Law of Attraction is constant and absolute. The magnetization of similar vibrations being pulled together happens organically, effortlessly and all the time. You do not have to think about the Law of Attraction to make it happen, it is actually always, in every moment, working to line up things of similar vibrations. The same as the Law of Gravity, you do not wake up and decide to use the Law of Gravity to walk on the floor today, the same way, you do not wake up and use the Law of Attraction to only attract things of like energy to you today. Imagine if just for a second gravity turned off and everything not attached to the ground started floating?! I mean fun!! … but not going to happen. The Law of Attraction is the same. It is always "on," and consistently responding to the vibration that you are emitting.

The Law of Attraction is Non-Judgmental. This can be both a blessing and a drawback because, as you've already learned, we are constantly communicating with the universe and it is constantly responding. Meaning if we are moving about our day and not being aware of how we are feeling and what we are putting out there, the universe will still be responding. There is no emotional attachment to lining you up with a speeding ticket because you were frustrated or a surprise gift because you were feeling lucky. It simply responds to your vibration, and there is always a lining up of similar vibrations in anything that happens in this universe. The Law of Attraction does not choose the things it lines you up with, that is your job.

The Law of Attraction is Inclusive. The universe has the ability to only say YES to what you are asking. As mentioned earlier, it has no judgment and therefore cannot deduce a yes or no answer. It will only and always respond yes. Remember here, we communicate through vibration not words, so if you say I want more money, but you are feeling fear because you don't have enough, the universe responds to your feeling and gives you more of "not enough." The universe will always give you more of what you are vibrationally asking for. This is the reason it is so important for you to be aware of how you are feeling.

I was coaching a couple that were very eager to sell their extra home and have the money in the bank. When we spoke they reported it had been on the market for over a year, they weren't happy with the real estate agent, it was stressful to spend money on anything in their life because they felt like they would run out if they didn't sell the house, business wasn't going well and they said they needed to sell the house to feel better. After they learned that the universe responds to how they are feeling about the situation and not what they are saying they want, they became aware of how discouraged they felt about selling the house and understood the universe can't possibly bring them more abundance when they feel so distressed over the situation. During our time together, they gradually began to shift how they felt about the house and about abundance in general, and with this realization and new thought pattern, life immediately got easier and less stressful. They continued to practice thoughts of relief and aligning with the abundance feelings they desired, and within 3 months, the house had sold and a new lucrative business opportunity was in the works.

KEY CONCEPTS TO REMEMBER

- You live in a vibrational universe
- Vibration is the foundation of the Law of Attraction
- We communicate to the universe through our emotions
- Each emotion carries its own frequency of vibration

This gives you a greater understanding why the law of attraction works and now it's time to learn how to make it work for you!

CHAPTER 2.

Know Your Power

In the last chapter you learned about your vibrational universe and how everything is vibration. That there is a constant communication or exchange of energy happening between you and everything else around you, and the Law of Attraction is simply responding to the vibrational frequency you are emitting by lining up similar frequencies. In this next chapter you will take it one step further and uncover your role in this cooperative universe. You will learn of your potential to be a conscious deliberate creation of your life, right now.

STOP BLAMING EVERYTHING ELSE

Decide right now to stop blaming other people or external conditions for your troubles. It is not the weather, not your parents, not your teachers, and not the government's fault that you don't have everything you want in your life. And it is not yours either. You have been unconsciously conditioned by society to believe certain facts about life that are false, to play small and to conform to ideas that suit the whole. Now, more than ever before, there is a shift in consciousness happening, where people like yourself are waking up to your own power. You are the one in charge of your own mind, of your own thoughts and control what you pay attention to. It is time to take responsibility for what you are experiencing and know that if something isn't the way you desire, you alone have the power to change it.

Three months ago Jessica, reached out to me for help in manifesting a new job. She hated her corporate workplace because there was so much negativity and she felt her boss was bullying her. Jessica was giving a lot of attention and power to the other people in her office, and after a couple sessions together she really started to understand that people were simply responding to her energy. If she felt that they were negative, that is how she would experience them. We practiced shifting the vibration towards more appreciation, and to her almost shock, Jessica began to enjoy the company of co-workers, reporting "my boss even complimented me today, AND I am up for a promotion!"

WHY YOU ARE HERE

You were born into this world, eager to be here. You came forth with the simple purpose to experience this life. To live, to feel and to be here. This physical world is the leading edge of all creation. This physical world is your playground, where you have the ability of turning thoughts to things. Where through your experiencing of life, you realize new thoughts and ideas and move the entire universe forward to a place it has never been before. Physical life on earth is the result and the basis for more and more universal expansion, to which there are no limits, and in every moment you are a part of this expansion.

THE ROLE OF THOUGHT IN CREATION

You have probably heard about creation being all about thoughts and what you think about, and yes thought plays a very important role, but I want you to understand that the thought is only the precursor to creation, not what actually influences the vibrational world around you. It begins with a thought and that thought translates to an emotion depending on what meaning you give that thought.

A thought is just a thing, it is objective...until you assign meaning to it, and then that meaning determines how you feel about it.

The meaning or judgment you choose to assign to a thought determines your emotional response to the thought. For example: two people can share the same thought that it is going to be a sunny hot weekend. To one

> *A thought is just a thing, it is objective... until you assign meaning to it, and then that meaning determines how you feel about it.*

person this means lots of fun playing outside, to another person it means no fun because they prefer to avoid the heat. The same thought can bring joy to one person

and grief to another. It is not the thought that holds the power, it is the meaning that you assign to the thought, and that is fully a conscious choice. This chapter is all about you understanding how your deliberate intent in this life can transform what you experience.

I have worked with a number of clients moving through divorce and typically this experience is deemed as one of the most stressful events in a person's life. When I got on the phone with Katie she talked about how she was dreading the court date, worrying she wouldn't get what she wanted and that she would just feel so angry with her ex. I asked "Who said that divorce has to be hard?" "Well that is what past experience of others has shown me." And then the ah-ha happens and she says, "But I am the creator of my own reality, I get to choose <u>how</u> I think about something, and it can be whatever I want – I want my divorce to be easy!" This was the beginning of Katie being deliberate about what meaning she was assigning to life events. Katie did experience a very smooth divorce, where she and her ex walked peacefully out of the court room together.

FROM UNCONSCIOUS TO CONSCIOUS: EXAMINING BELIEFS

Most of our beliefs are formed within us from a young age as our parents and mentors genuinely guide us about what is right and wrong and real. They believe they are passing on facts about life, and this is how you receive them, but in reality beliefs and truths are subjective, and every individual has a choice in what they believe is true and real, which ultimately creates their experience.

When you were a child maybe you were repeatedly told to make sure you always lock the doors and windows at home, which sends the message that the world is a scary and dangerous place, and you must always be cautious and careful. This is going to generate a feeling of fear within you as a child, which is what you will emit to the universe and to which the Law of Attraction will respond. The universe will naturally line up fearful experiences for you, which you then observe as evidence of a scary world. The universe will support your beliefs, irrelevant of whether they serve you or not.

Why is it, you think, that two different people can live in exactly the same town and yet believe different

truths about it? Ask one person and they report it is a great place to live, ask another person and it is an awful place to live. It is the same town, what is the truth? There is not one right or wrong belief about anything; there are many right beliefs. Beliefs are a choice. This is part of our foundational freedom as we enter into this physical world; we have the choice and freedom to believe anything we want, about anything we want.

WE CAN CHANGE OUR BELIEFS

Now that you are aware how your beliefs and thoughts affect what you experience, you hold the power to guide your beliefs in a way that supports your desires. The process to change a belief is incredibly straightforward. A belief is simply a thought you keep thinking, so if you want to hold a new belief about something, start thinking a new thought about it. Ask yourself "What do I want to be true for me?" and start practicing that thought instead of the old one. With time you will form a new belief, and the universe will respond by giving you evidence of this. (To download your creating new beliefs worksheet, visit ginnygane. com/funfreestuff)

Years ago I was in the beginning stages of building my coaching practice and feeling defeated, like I was going nowhere fast. When I asked myself what I wanted to be true, the answer was successful, which made me realize I didn't believe that I was successful. Ah-hah! I couldn't possibly experience success if I didn't first believe that I was successful. Most people, and I am guessing anyone who is reading this book, knows that until you believe it, it will not happen. That belief is an essential component to the achievement of any goal or desire. When you believe it to be true, it will be, and within one week of talking to myself and viewing myself as a successful coach now, I had manifested two new clients.

During your childhood and maybe still to this day, you may have heard things like, "you have to work hard to be successful," "good things never last," "life is hard." I want you to realize that these are only beliefs which have been unconsciously conditioned in you by society, and you have the power to change them starting right now. The time of unconsciousness for you is now a thing of the past. You are the deliberate creator of your life.

A belief is simply a thought you keep thinking and therefore building new beliefs is all about consistently practicing a new thought.

What do you want to believe? Write it down, tape it to your wall and continue to repeat this to yourself until you begin to feel it and then have fun observing all the evidence to support it in your life.

It is always such a joy for me to witness my clients' journeys to really seeing, in their own lives how changing their beliefs, changes their realities. One of my favourite stories came recently from working with a woman who felt overwhelmed in

A belief is simply a thought you keep thinking and therefore building new beliefs is all about consistently practicing a new thought.

her home and business life. We came up with the affirmation, "I create a life of ease," which she would continually repeat throughout her days, whenever she felt overwhelmed. After one week, we jumped on a call and she was so excited how easy everything was feeling, dealing with clients was effortless, getting up for the day felt easier, and then another week passed and she found herself peacefully enjoying the day before her vacation as everything was already packed an in order, something that had never happened before. Your reality will reflect what you decide to be true.

THE ULTIMATE POWER OF FOCUS

This chapter is all about getting to know your own power. The basis of your power comes from the fact that there is no one else inside your head, telling you how or what to think. There are loads of people outside of you, trying to guide you in ways that please them, but you are the one with the final decision. You get to decide which thoughts you accept to be true and which ones you dismiss. Being deliberate in your life is about consciously making choices. You have the power to direct your focus in any way that you desire, and THIS is the foundation to deliberate creation.

Energy flows where attention goes
– **Michael Beckwith**

As you learn to focus your attention on the things that you want more of in your life, you begin to receive more of the things you want in your life. You leverage the Law of Attraction by becoming aware of which thoughts you are thinking, how those thoughts create an emotional response in you, and then choosing to give more attention to the thoughts that cause you to feel positive. We have over 60 thousand thoughts in one day and 90% of those thoughts are about the same thing. Understanding that thoughts and emotions create your reality, it is obvious why so many of you are getting the same thing over and over. You must transition more of your thoughts to be about what you want in order to attract what you want.

What most people don't understand is their power in choosing thought. Thinking has become an addiction, where we just can't seem to control our thoughts, but thoughts do not just think us. We have the conscious choice to give attention to something or not. Yes of course there are random thoughts that pop up within our mind, but if you are aware, you will notice that you can choose to let that thought pass or choose to keep your focus there. This process of focusing thought may seem challenging at first, but that is only because you have practiced one way of thinking for so many years, and the more practiced a thought, the easier it is to access. From the example above, the more and more my client practiced the thought that she creates a life of ease, the easier it was for that to be her "go to" thought. Eventually your mind will fall into the new thought first, leaving the old conditioning to be a thing of the past.

There is an example I use with many new clients when we start working together, in how the thought patterns that you practice most, seem more natural. The same way a truck driving down the same path on a dirt road year after year would develop a rut to fit the tire, you have created a mental track for your mind that is so easy and familiar to drive in. Like the tire slips into the well-worn rut, your mind simply falls back into old thought patterns. Anyone can choose to be more deliberate in their life and easily manifest desires, they just have to consistently drive down a different part of the road.

You are the Answer

The incredible beauty of this whole Law of Attraction concept is that you, and you alone have the power to control what vibration you send out to the universe. You are the only one inside your head that can choose to direct your focus. You get to choose the meaning you assign to your thoughts, which translate to your emotion, which leads to the vibration that you are offering to the universe. The whole process is that simple. Learn to focus in a way that generates positive emotion within you. Deliberately directing your focus is a skill, and like any skill, it is a journey to mastery. Throughout the next chapters, I am going to walk you through the steps to take to begin your journey to mastery. I am so excited for you; it is going to be such a fun ride!

CHAPTER 3.

Release the Struggle and Live a Life of Ease

One of my favourite stories from the teachings of Abraham is when Esther and Jerry go white water rafting. It was the two of them, and another couple along with a high school wrestling team on a bus, which I'm sure would have been quite the entertaining scene. They drove in a bus up along the side of the raging river that they were soon to be floating down, and when Esther saw the raging waters and sharp boulders, she suddenly had this great idea. "How about you put our raft in the water at the end, after all the rapids?" To which the leader laughed and replied, "But then you would miss the fun of the ride down the stream."

Our life is like that stream and when you are born into this world, you put your boat in the water. The power of the current will naturally carry you forward through life and as a young child you float easily and effortlessly down the stream. Then as you get older, you begin to have conscious thought and those thoughts are like putting your oars in the water. You can have downstream (non-resistant) thoughts that help steer you along the path to what you want or you can have upstream (resistant) thoughts, which are like you paddling against the powerful stream. The thing that is really important for you to know is that nothing you want is upstream. Knowing this, you want to be able to always choose thoughts that point you downstream and bring you quicker and easier to your desires.

This process requires you to be constantly aware of your thoughts, and if a thought is resistant or non-resistant. In other words, does the thought point your raft upstream; against the natural flow, or downstream; with the natural flow? So how do you know if a thought is upstream or downstream?

YOUR EMOTIONAL GUIDANCE SYSTEM

We are in every moment being guided by that broader non-physical energy we call Source. Like you have previously learned, we interact with Source energy through emotion. It is our emotions that are constantly and consistently guiding us on our path downstream. You can tell if a thought is upstream or downstream (resistant or not) by how it feels to you. Your emotions are your indicator. Good feeling thoughts take you downstream closer to what you want, and bad feeling thoughts keep your raft pointed upstream away from what you want. In the last chapter you uncovered your power of choice. You have the power to choose the way you feel in any moment about any thing. Now you know that good feeling thoughts lead you towards your desires, while bad feeling thoughts hold you away from your desires.

THE QUICKEST WAY TO WHAT YOU WANT

The quickest way for you to get to your dream house or dream partner is to let go of the oars and trust the power of the stream.

The energy that creates worlds and gives you life is the same energy that is guiding your path. There is something divine and all knowing about source energy, and when you trust this energy, you let go of resistance. You let go of trying. And when you stop fighting against the current of the stream, you are powerfully and quickly moved toward what you want. After you learn to consistently go with the flow, you can then train your thoughts to navigate your path down the stream, avoiding possible boulders along the way. Source energy, from the non-physical vantage point knows and can see your path of least resistance, and is always guiding you there.

The quickest way for you to get to your dream house or dream partner is to let go of the oars and trust the power of the stream.

Have you ever heard of a couple who have been trying for years to have a child with no luck, and then they stop trying and maybe decide to adopt, and a month later they find out they are pregnant? Or how often you meet a romantic partner when you aren't even looking? When you aren't efforting or trying to control the path, everything easily falls into place.

This path of least resistance is the experience you are yearning for, yet not the one you are conditioned to follow. You are trained to work really hard, put in the long hours, struggle and paddle upstream to get to what you want, but I am telling you right now that the path to living your dream life can be one of ease. You can choose to go with the flow or you can choose to paddle upstream. Either way the power of the stream will bring you to your desire, the only difference is your experience of the ride along the way.

RELIEF AS AN ESSENTIAL EMOTION

Part of living a resistance free life is about always reaching for the feeling of relief. Ultimately you want to spend as much time in the high vibrations of love and appreciation as possible, but the goal is not to instantly jump straight there. The smoothest and (longest-lasting) path to the high vibrations is a gradual one, and this process is called moving up the emotional scale. Take a look at a visual representation of the emotional scale, which I first learned of from Abraham-Hicks.

Emotional Scale

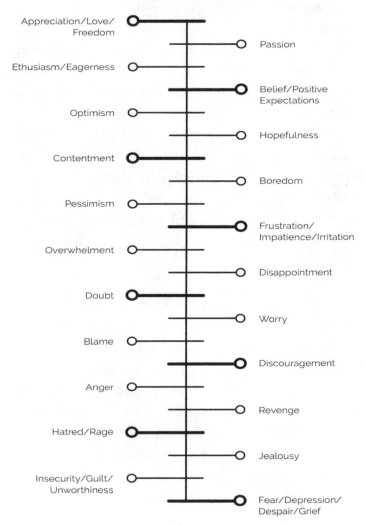

1. Relief is the emotion that will gradually move you up the emotional scale.
2. It is always possible to find a thought that will bring some element of relief.
3. You determine what thought feels like relief by asking yourself "Does this feel a little better?"
4. Reaching for a feeling of relief does not always mean you are reaching for a positive emotion. If you are feeling jealousy, reaching for a thought that brings anger is actually movement up the emotional scale, and releases resistance.
5. Feeling any amount of relief lessens your vibrational resistance and begins to turn your raft downstream.

THE RELATIONSHIP BETWEEN YOU AND SOURCE

There is a foundational concept to being able to masterfully leverage the Law of Attraction in that you must take care of yourself first. And in fact, tending to how you are feeling first is the best way you can truly impact the people and the world around you. Keep in mind that the universe is only responding to your vibration, so paying attention and fine-tuning your own vibration will allow you to attract what you want.

You come from a broader non-physical energy that is called Source, and when you were born into this physical world part of that greater non-physical energy became focused through you in this physical world. This is what you generally define as who you are. Part of this energy is given a body, your body, and a name, your name, and voila you are you. But there is actually so much more to you than you can see. There is a larger part of your energy that stays focused in the non-physical world, and remains a part of that greater one divine intelligence that we call Source energy.

Source energy is the divine purely positive love energy that everything comes from and returns to. Our life here on this planet is merely a short stint in the continually expanding universe as a whole. Who you really are is eternal. Yes your body will only last so many years on this planet, but then, who you really are inside that body will return to the larger part of you and all of you will be once again focused as Source energy.

The part of your energy that is focused in this world, experiences life's events and takes on a certain perspective, while the greater part of your energy remains focused in the non-physical and holds a different perspective. The non-physical vantage point is unconditional and knows the absoluteness of your worthiness because they know who you really are. The awareness that you come from a place of pure positive love energy never leaves, and that perspective is always flowing to and through you in your physical form. From the perspective of Source you are always loved, valued and appreciated. Source is always high vibing.

FIND ALIGNMENT WITH THE PERSPECTIVE OF SOURCE

In order for you in your physical form to feel the high emotions of love, joy and appreciation, you must align your perspective to that of Source. You must feel the way about yourself, as Source does. When the two perspectives are in alignment, there is no vibrational gap and you feel positive emotion. Positive emotion is the signal to you that something is true and that source feels the same way. Negative emotion is the signal to you that your thought is not in alignment with Source and therefore not true.

Remember back to when your last relationship was ending, and once again for whatever reason it didn't work out and you are single again. You think to yourself, "What's wrong with me, why can't I make a relationship work?" which obviously makes you feel crappy. This thought makes you feel bad because from the vantage point of Source, it is not true. If you, just for a moment would step back and take the perspective of Source, which unconditionally accepts that you are doing your best on your path, you would see there is nothing wrong with you, and if you would just stop beating yourself up and feeling bad for a few moments, you would find relief and shift your vibration to allow in the next best relationship for you. The ideal relationship is waiting for you, but you are stuck in the vibration of you not being good enough and therefore cannot possibly line up with what you want.

You can find relief from any negative thought that you have. Here is an example of working your way gradually up the emotional scale after someone said something mean to you and hurt your feelings.

People don't like me, it makes me feel sad, like I should be better. I don't understand why they don't like me, maybe I did something I don't know about, or maybe there was just a miscommunication, maybe they were just having a bad day. I guess there could be lots of reasons they said something mean. It doesn't have to mean they don't like me, I get to decide what it means. I know there are some people that do like me, I don't have to make this such a big deal, I like feeling easy about things, I'm getting better and finding relief when I want to, I feel a little better already, and I know more and more good thoughts will come to me now. What I really want is for me to feel good about me and not care what other people think so much. It actually doesn't matter because I can't control them, I can only control how I feel. I feel really good knowing that I can choose how I feel, and I don't have to let this bother me. What he said to me probably has nothing to do with me anyways. I feel so much better now. I love this process!

> *The most important feeling to ever reach for is the feeling of relief.*

So now you know the most important feeling to ever reach for is the feeling of relief.

If you let this be your guiding principle for leveraging the Law of Attraction, you will be constantly moving on the path of least resistance, toward greater alignment with Source energy. This alignment feels like extraordinary ease in your life. You start to get all the green lights, you begin to have the best customer service experiences, the person you have been meaning to get in touch with calls you out of the blue, the problem at work organically works itself out, and you see 11:11 a lot or double numbers everywhere you look. You have control over what you experience in your life because you create your reality by what you choose to think and feel. Pay attention to you first, feel your way towards more and more relief and watch as your spectacular path unfolds before you.

KEY CONCEPTS TO REMEMBER

- The path of least resistance is a path without struggle, like floating downstream
- When you are "trying" you are going against the natural flow of life
- Your emotions are always guiding you on the path of least resistance
- Negative feeling thoughts equal resistance (upstream)
- Positive feeling thoughts allow in your desires effortlessly (downstream)

- The emotion you always want to reach for is relief
- When you share the same perspective of you as Source does, you are in alignment
- Feeling more and more relief will lead you to alignment

CHAPTER 4.

Manifest Any Desire
in 3 Simple Steps

H ave you noticed that sometimes, wait, most of the time, we as humans like to complicate things? There is something about the idea of things being simple that is just too easy. That's it! We are conditioned that everything needs to be hard and when it is easy, we question if it is right or not. Ask yourself right now if you hold the expectation that certain things in your life are going to be easy or hard. Do you expect that meeting the love of your life will be easy? Do you think getting an extra hundred thousand dollars will be hard? From everything you have learned so far, you know that these beliefs you have about things are simply conditioned in you, and when you become aware of them, you have the power to create something new or start telling a new story. Right now I want you to start telling yourself the story that manifestations are easy for you and they happen effortlessly all the time. You are going to learn specific tools to practice in the next chapter, but for right now, open up your mind to the idea that manifesting is easy.

Ease is one of the primary themes that I choose to carry and create throughout my life. I want things for me to flow, I love the feeling of everything working out for me, and I have deliberately created my life to be this way. This is why I came up with these three really simple steps that you can apply to anything that you desire to manifest within your life. These steps will absolutely work for anything you want, so dream big and have fun!

To download your own free summary of 3 Super Simple Steps, visit ginnygane.com/funfreestuff

STEP ONE – CLEARLY DEFINE WHAT YOU WANT

One of the first things I talk about with all of my clients is what they want. There is a reason that you are reading this book, there is something you want, that you feel you do not have, and bringing clarity to what it is, will dramatically move your journey toward it forward. My close friend and successful coach, Cassie Parks says it the best when she talks about clarifying what you want. She says, "Clarity is a fundamental key to getting what you want. The problem is most people think they have clarity when there is still exploration to do. The question that leads to deeper clarity is what do I really want?" It is actually a skill to learn to listen to your own inner voice when you ask yourself this. There are so many societal pressures that influence your choices and most of the time you don't even realize it is happening.

You have been taught to look for answers outside yourself and trained away from paying attention to your inner guidance system, so even just answering this question freely can be a challenge.

We face so many decisions, mostly small ones, throughout our day to day that we can be practicing this skill of asking ourselves what we want. You are making dinner decisions, thinking about your partner, or the kids, or the cost of different things or what's available, or what is the quickest, next time, stop and ask yourself, what do I <u>want</u> to eat tonight? Determining plans for the weekend can sometimes even be overwhelming, but stop and ask yourself, "if I was only responsible for me, and not pleasing anyone else, what would I really want?" Constantly checking in to your desires with this question, will teach you to trust yourself and know what the right answer for you emotionally feels like.

Here are a few questions you can ask yourself to gain a better understanding of what it is you really want:

1. A magic genie will grant you 3 wishes, what are they?
2. If there were no way that you could fail, what would you want to achieve?
3. What is the thing that you are scared to want?

THE JOURNEY TO CLARITY

Clarity is a journey. It is kind of like a smaller scale life journey where you are constantly determining your preferences and moving toward them. Although sometimes you get stuck giving so much attention to where you are that you cannot be the creator of new life experiences. The same thing happens in your search for clarity, you observe an experience of not knowing what you want and then get stuck there. When you feel the emotion of confusion, it can be a time of celebration! It means you are being called to more clarity about the

You are being guided by your emotions to the right path for you, ever changing and always unfolding,

subject, because if there were nothing more to clarify, there would be no vibrational discord or confusion. Source wouldn't let you feel good where you are if there wasn't already more waiting for you in your vibrational reality.

The problem arises with your constant observation of the confusion, and in addition to that, trying to find clarity and solve the problem. Just like we talked about earlier in the book, when you are trying to do anything, you are paddling upstream against the natural flow of life.

You are being guided by your emotions to the right path for you, ever changing and always unfolding, so relax along the way and trust in your process of uncovering greater levels of clarity.

Another aspect of clarity being a dynamic thing is that as you change, what you want changes too. Think back to when you were 10 years old and the most important thing in the world to you was your Barbies or ninja turtles. And then in high school, making sure you were wearing the coolest outfit was top priority, followed by finding an income source so you could move out of your parents' house. Where you are now, your priorities and what you want are different. Thank goodness! Does taking this bigger picture view allow you to feel an element of appreciation for the unfolding and the changing of desires? Allowing yourself to be wherever you are right now on your path to clarity will open up the space for more clarity to come in.

You can only activate one vibrational side of a subject at one time. Meaning if you feel confused, it is impossible to line up with clarity because they are two different vibrations. In order to allow in clarity you must get off of the confusion vibration, which is where your deliberate awareness takes stage front and center. First step is being aware that you are in confusion, acknowledge that this emotion is present in order to guide you towards more clarity. Next step is to either talk yourself up the emotional scale by using phrases that bring relief to you or totally distract yourself by bringing your attention to a subject you have no resistance on.

STATEMENTS OF RELIEF

- Things are always working out for me
- I am open to feeling different about this topic
- Everything is temporary and I will feel different soon
- I don't have to figure this out right now
- It feels better to leave this one up to the universe to figure out
- I can just let it be
- It's easier to just go with the flow

IDEAS TO DISTRACT YOURSELF

- Hilarious YouTube pet clips
- Inspiring audio or video segments
- A walk around the block or in the forest
- Gardening

- Netflix show
- Cooking

YOU CAN FEEL CLARITY

When you are clear about something, you know it. Clarity is a palatable feeling in your body, which happens when you and the Source within you are in alignment. This alignment is what you are reaching for and you know you are there when you have an idea and every part of you is saying Hell Yes! If you aren't feeling this kind of absolute knowing clarity, continue to allow more momentum to come into your life. Continue to be aware of evidence entering your reality and guiding you towards greater and greater clarity. Enjoy and embrace every part of your journey to uncovering what you really want.

STEP TWO - CLARIFY THE FEELING

You are already keenly aware that we communicate to the universe through our emotions versus through our words. So for example when you offer a desire to the universe saying "I want more money" or "I want to lose weight" it is not the words you use that are important, but how you feel about what you are saying. Two people could say the exact same phrase of "I want more money;" one person feels excited about having more money while another feels distressed that they don't have enough. They use the same words but the universe will respond in two completely different ways to each of them because they each FEEL different about what they are saying.

This is why it is so vital for you to clarify the emotion you are after. You believe that you want the thing because you want the thing, when in reality; you want the thing because of how you think it will make you feel. You want the new job so that you can earn more money and spend more time at home with the kids, when the core of the matter is you want to feel freedom in your life. You tell yourself, I will be really successful when I have the new job, I will be happy when I fall in love, I will accept myself when I lose the weight. And you can go that journey, you can do life like that, but that is the hard way. Those are the paths filled with struggle and hard work and sacrifice and I want you to experience ease and joy and feel the power of the energy that creates worlds flow through you. To access this flow you must feel the feeling before you see the physical evidence of your desire, and then, it is the law, you will experience the physical reality of what you desire.

So refer back to your answers to the question "What do I really want?" Open up your mind to the experiencing of this thing that you want, and tap into the feeling that you are getting because of it. Create a visualization in your mind of you having what you want or think of someone else you know that has what you want, and identify the feelings you are associating with having it. When you are clear about the feeling you really want to feel, you have the power to activate that feeling now, and let the Law of Attraction do all the heavy lifting of manifesting the physical version of your dreams.

STEP THREE - ALIGNMENT

The entire foundation of leveraging the Law of Attraction rests upon you finding alignment with the Source within you.

The source within you places no conditions on its complete acceptance and love of who you are. When you share this same perspective of yourself, there is alignment. When you feel excitement about an idea, it feels good to you because Source agrees and there is no vibrational gap. When you feel like a failure, it feels bad because Source does not agree and there is a vibrational gap. Constant awareness of your relationship with Source allows you to make choices to easily move down the path of least resistance.

The entire foundation of leveraging the Law of Attraction rests upon you finding alignment with the Source within you.

It is like when you are driving down the highway and you move too far over the outside line and the bumps on the road make this crazy loud sound to remind you to get back on the road. Your emotions are constantly doing the same thing for you, you start to think a thought that is not aligned with source, a negative emotion pops up to say, oh nope, the things you want aren't over here. These are the situations where you learn to reach for a feeling that brings you relief. Relief gets you back on the road, pointed in the right direction and eventually you begin to get going faster again and feel more and more positive emotion.

ALIGN WITH A SPECIFIC FEELING

Deliberate creation is all about feeling the way you want to feel in the future, in this moment. This moment carries equal potential for you to feel what you want, as does the same moment in the future. You have the power to feel how you want to feel by deliberately choosing your focus. One way to do this can be aligning with a specific feeling. Let's say for example, you desire to manifest a dream partner and have already identified you want this for the feeling of being appreciated. In order for you to let the Law of Attraction do the work, you need to find a way to feel appreciated now and then the partner will match this vibration. To activate the vibration of appreciation in your life, you could begin by giving attention to things that you appreciate right now.

The Law of Attraction makes it really easy for you to build momentum one way or another. With only 17 seconds of focus on a thought, the Law of Attraction will bring you another thought that is similar in vibration and then another and another. This is how momentum builds. The key is in which way you are allowing this momentum to grow, is it towards thoughts that feel good or thoughts that feel bad, because the universe holds no judgment either way.

Another way to align with a specific feeling is to recall events in your past that caused you to feel the desired way. You have a desire to feel more depth and connection in your life, so ask yourself, when was a time in my past when I felt this way. The simple act of recalling the memory will activate, in the present moment, the vibration you are looking for. It is the present moment that holds all of creation's power for you. What you are focusing on and feeling right now, is what you are creating for your future. The more you can deliberately find ways to align with the feelings you want to be feeling, the quicker and easier, your desires become your reality.

POWER OF PRACTICE

It is the case with all of these steps that the more you experience and practice the skills of each, the easier it all becomes. When you are learning to drive a car, at the beginning you consciously think of every detail and it takes a lot of focus, but eventually it becomes natural and you sometimes even find yourself driving home without thinking. The more often you ask yourself "What do I really want?" the more you learn through experience what clarity feels like in your body and mind. The more you ask yourself how does this feel to me, the more you tune into your individual emotional guidance system, learn what different emotions feel like, and how they are guiding you. The more you practice the vibration you want to feel, you get more familiar with it and it ultimately becomes second nature to you. Consistent application and practice of these three simple steps will allow you to line up with your desires faster and easier than you can even imagine!

CHAPTER 5.

Key LOA Skills and Action Steps for Successful Manifestations

---

"Learning is an experience. Everything else is just information." - **Einstein**

To learn something new, one must practice the skills involved. It seems so obvious, and we apply this to most everything we do in life like learning to walk, play a sport, learn an instrument or a language, we understand that we have to practice the new skills to master the subject. But what about when it comes to life stuff? Are you ever taught in school how to easily handle relationships in your life? How to communicate effectively? These essential skills that are fundamental to a successful life are actually not taught to you and therefore life itself ends up being the game and your practice field.

THE DIFFERENCE BETWEEN KNOWING AND LIVING IT

There is a massive difference between knowing something and really knowing something. You know what I mean? In other words, you can read something and know it and you can do something and know it. There are these different levels of understanding things that seem to continue to develop and get deeper and deeper. It feels like our capacity to understand concepts is almost limitless. We keep learning more and more and there is always more to learn.

I like to term two different experiences of knowledge as intellectual knowledge and experiential knowledge. I am quite certain I did not invent those terms, but that is how I know them. Intellectual knowledge being when you read or listen to something or someone tells you a piece of information or fact, like when you add two plus two, it equals four. Or when you approach a stop sign, you know in your mind you are required to stop your car. These are examples of intellectual knowledge. You fully understand the concepts in your mind. When you are asked to complete an addition question in your homework or when you are driving a car and stop at a stop sign, these are examples of experiential knowledge, where you have a different and deeper understanding of the concept because you have physically experienced it. As you physically experience something, it eventually becomes a knowing within you. You don't have to think about it, you just know it.

Your mastery of a skill parallels the development of your experiential knowledge. You can read all about the Law of Attraction in books and listen to audios but unless you apply the concepts to your life, you will never really know and understand the principles. Throughout this chapter, I am going to share with you four skills that are core to powerfully leveraging the Law of Attraction and give you action steps to take in your own life in order to develop your experiential knowledge.

AWARENESS

Where it all begins. I think of awareness as synonymous with consciousness, in that you have the ability to step back, and observe yourself and your own mind. When you are aware, you move through life with a purpose behind your actions, a level of understanding about why things are happening and maintain a deliberate intent. On our podcast, Manifest It Now (http://manifestitnowshow.com) fellow LOA savvy coach Cassie Parks and I are always talking about awareness. You'll hear us laugh about how it comes up in pretty much every discussion, saying, "The first step is awareness…" And it is true! In all of the skills and concepts you will learn, you will use and develop your awareness. Your awareness of your desire for something more is ultimately what brought you to where you are right now reading this book.

It is your awareness that allows you to know when you want something different. Your emotional guidance system offers you both positive and negative emotion, but you must be aware of your emotions in order to adjust accordingly. Maybe one evening you are all ready to go out and you find yourself impatiently standing at the door, tapping your watch, waiting for your partner to be ready so you can leave. Someone with a practiced sense of awareness would catch themselves feeling impatient, acknowledge that it does not feel good, and course correct their focus onto something else that makes them feel positive (possibly the friends that they are looking forward to seeing). A person who is less aware will just move through their evening responding to what is happening around them, letting their external situation dictate their emotions.

Actually, this is what most of the population does. They observe something happening in their environment and base their emotional response on this. You see on the news, the transportation system is striking and you let this make you feel upset, or oppositely, you take a walk in the park, see a child laughing and playing and this causes you to feel joy. You are letting your physical surroundings determine your emotions, which is a very tricky game to play because you cannot and will not ever be able to control everything that happens around you. If you live this way you are asking for all the conditions around you to always please you. And the same conditions do not please all of the diverse people in our world, this is why you have been given the power to choose and focus on your own preferences, so that you can create the best reality for you, independent of what is best for someone else, and this begins with your awareness. Your awareness is vital to your transformation and expansion in this life.

HOW TO PRACTICE AND DEVELOP YOUR AWARENESS

I want you to make the connection between what you are thinking about and focusing on and what you are feeling. I want you to learn through experience that when you are focused on what you want, you will feel positive emotion and when you are giving attention to the lack of what you want, you will feel negative emotion.

The cool thing about how this works is that although sometimes it is challenging to know what you are thinking about all the time, it is pretty hard to miss a strong emotional reaction. You usually know when you are really happy or feeling in the dumps; thus the magic of our emotional guidance system. Your task today is to observe when you are feeling really good or when you are feeling bad, stop yourself in those moments and ask, "what am I thinking about?" This is such a simple practice but extremely powerful in creating the awareness of the connection. When you are aware of something the way it is, you have a starting line for where you are headed. Continue to do this everyday this week, actually recording on paper what thoughts are correlating with what emotions. As you allow yourself to bring awareness to your focus in this way, you will easily realize you spend a lot of time thinking about the same things, and then from there it is an easy question, is this what I want to be creating more of in my life? Start with the awareness of where you are, and then you can learn to guide your focus in ways that serve you and everyone around you the most.

APPRECIATION

Let's dive into the magic behind gratitude and appreciation by first identifying the difference between them. The two terms are so easily interchangeable in common dialogue, but I feel there is a very important difference between the two, which can make or break a successful gratitude practice. The difference of emotion. I define gratitude as something we are thankful for in our lives, but the acknowledgement of being thankful for it is pretty much where it ends. People ask you what you are grateful for and you can likely list off your health, parents, houses, and friends...with not too much meaning attached to it.

Alternatively, when I think of appreciation, I think of why I am grateful for a certain thing. I am grateful for my health because it lets me be active in athletics, climb mountains, and have incredible adventure experiences, which ultimately makes me feel free.

The reasons WHY you are grateful for something equals appreciation.

In fact, research by Professor Nancy Fagley of Rutgers University found appreciation and gratitude seem to be both strongly connected to happiness, but her results suggest appreciation is twice as significant as gratitude in determining overall satisfaction with life. When I recently attended a live Abraham-Hicks workshop, Abraham was clear in identifying that appreciation and gratitude are not the same thing and appreciation is absolutely more

> *The reasons WHY you are grateful for something equals appreciation.*

powerful in leveraging the Law of Attraction and your deliberate creation. Which makes sense because you know that it is all about emotion, and so anything that is going to activate a stronger emotion is going to have more manifesting power in the universal language.

THE APPRECIATION VIBRATION

One of the main reasons why activating the vibration of appreciation is so powerful is because the frequency is very close to the highest possible vibration, which is that of unconditional love. When you are in complete alignment with your inner being or Source, you are in the vibration of love. This is the most allowing or resistance free space to be and where the Law of Attraction is bringing you what you want!

There is always something to be appreciative of. From wherever you are, wherever you are, you can find at the least, one small thing to flow appreciation towards. All you need is to find one thing, focus your pure attention there for at least 17 seconds and the Law of Attraction will bring you another thought of similar frequency. This is how you build momentum and begin a positive upward spiral of thoughts and therefore emotions. As you deliberately choose to focus on appreciation, you will begin to shift your vibration and the universe will respond by bringing you more things and experiences in your life to be appreciative of.

I had one client begin a daily practice of appreciation where every morning she would sit up in bed and write a list of what she was appreciative of in her life. After only one week, she reported back that she felt a cloud had been lifted off her life, she was enjoying her days, it was easier to see the positive, it was so much easier to see what she was grateful for in her life, a stranger had bought her coffee for her, she received an unexpected $200, her daughter didn't get into trouble, she overall felt like everything was working out for her. All in just one week! The universe responds immediately when you begin to shift your dominant vibration.

HOW TO PRACTICE AND DEVELOP APPRECIATION

The easiest way to start to practice this skill is the same as in the example above. Your morning time, right when you open your eyes and begin thought again, is the most important time in your day because it is like a fresh slate. While you sleep, you stop thought and therefore stop resistance and are flowing free, so when you wake up, you have the opportunity to powerfully set up where your vibration is going to start off. Choosing to think in your head or write down things that you are appreciative of at this time is an awesome idea!

A few other ways you can practice appreciation are by telling someone else something you appreciate about them, looking in the mirror when you are brushing your teeth and saying thank you to you, thinking about what your favourite thing to be appreciative of is or having a conversation with someone else about appreciation. The more attention and energy you can bring to it, the more momentum you will build and the faster the universe can respond.

"In the vibration of appreciation all things come to you. You don't have to make anything happen. From what you are living, amplify the things you appreciate so that it is the dominate vibration you are offering and then only those things that are a vibrational match to that can come to you. Then sit back and know, "You ain't seen nothing yet!!!"

– Esther Hicks,
Money, and the Law of Attraction

SELF-LOVE

Self-love is defined as regard for one's own well-being and happiness. In other words, how we take care of ourselves, both our physical and emotional selves. This seemingly little element is actually paramount to anything we do in our lives. Unfortunately, traditional beliefs about taking care of ourselves often fall under the category of selfish. Still, today there is an underlying pressure or judgment in our culture that implies we are better or valued more if we sacrifice our own needs to put others first. Selfish to me, means making happiness and feeling good the priority and this is a good thing.

It is my belief that every act is a selfish one, and there is nothing you can do in this world that isn't serving you in some way. Maybe you will tell me you volunteer and give your time, you give away money to charities, you help people in need, and you are doing it to help them and make them feel good. Yes, you are helping them, but ultimately you are doing it for you. You do it to make YOU feel good and satisfy your need for something, whether it is to feel useful, have a purpose, be generous or kind.

You see, every action we take is selfishly motivated, so it's time to let yourself take care of you first. We all deserve it. We are all selfish beings, and we must begin to embrace this instead of casting a dark eye on "selfish" actions. We must lead and take care of ourselves first to be who we are meant to be in this world; and as consciousness as a whole awakens, many are realizing that taking care of ourselves first is, in fact, the only way we can truly, in turn take care of others.

You grow more as individuals and consequently as a whole by being true to yourself and living your truth than you ever will by giving up what you believe to satisfy another's belief or want.

There is so much good that comes out of people being selfish and taking care of themselves. You are here on this planet to be who you are, every single different person here is different for a reason, and this contrast and diversity inspires and creates expansion.

You grow more as individuals and consequently as a whole by being true to yourself and living your truth than you ever will by giving up what you believe to satisfy another's belief or want.

Being able to fully leverage the Law of Attraction requires alignment with your inner being, which is nearly impossible if you are denying part of who you are or what you want. This is why it is so important to start taking care of yourself by practicing what we are terming here as "Self-Love."

Can you really love another if you cannot first love yourself?

You cannot give something away unless you first possess it, right? How can you give someone a birthday gift unless you first have something to give them? How is it possible to give true respect to others if you do not have it first for yourself? Love is the same way. You must BE love before you can purely love others.

To me, loving yourself simply means acknowledging and maintaining an awareness of who you already truly are. At your core, you are pure positive love energy. So you don't need to learn anything new, simply uncover who you really are. There may be times when you feel depleted after just listening to someone else's trouble or problem. But when you are connected to and being your true self, you organically flow love, kindness, and compassion towards yourself and others. The key is in getting and staying in this state. You practice self-love, so you are able to be your best self to help others in the best way you can. You CAN give, love, and serve unconditionally, but it requires you to be connected with your true self first, which first requires self-care.

You must find and maintain connection with your true self in order to truly help inspire connection and empowerment in others. You can think of it as though you have two selves. You and the you that you talk to. Right? Become aware of how often you talk to yourself, telling yourself "You did a great job," or "That wasn't the best thing to say," or "Remember to do that"–well who is talking to whom in these situations? You have already learned how you have your inner being, true self, Source energy, and having your conscious thinking mind or egoic self. Your true self is pure positive energy and is eternal. Remember your true self knows your value and worthiness, there is no question as to whether you are good enough or not, you ALWAYS are. Your mind self is how you experience and perceive reality in this physical world, and is often times very critical and judgmental. When you can bring the perspective of your mind self to align with the eternal perspective of your true self, you are practicing real self love and can live unconditionally in this world. This alignment of the two perspectives creates experiences that feel magical in our reality. When you find consistent alignment with your true self, you allow access to a never-ending stream of well-being and abundance...and you feel unbelievably awesome!

WHY PRACTICING LOVE TOWARD YOURSELF WILL TRANSFORM YOU

Your external reality is a direct reflection of your internal reality. If you make your internal reality full of love, your external reality will reflect that. The more you love yourself, the more love you will see and receive. The universe can only treat you as well as you treat yourself. If you are looking to experience something different in the world, let's say you want to feel more appreciated in your work, you have to change your internal reality first! You must find ways to appreciate your work, and you will begin to receive more appreciation from everywhere else, it is the law.

The most important thing you can do to help the people you love is take care of yourself—like our trusted stewardess's clear request to please put your oxygen mask on first before assisting others.

HOW TO PRACTICE AND DEVELOP SELF-LOVE

The single most powerful self-love practice you will ever do is talking to yourself in a positive way. You think more than sixty thousand thoughts per day–you are always in your head, listening to what you say. Remember if you hear something enough times, you start to accept the thought as truth or a belief. A belief is simply a thought you keep thinking, so what are you thinking about for the majority of your sixty thousand thoughts? Are you more supportive of yourself or more disapproving? Are you more positive or negative, more kind or harsh, more forgiving or less? The harder or more negative you are toward yourself, the harder and more negative your life experience is, which is the surest way to cut off the flow of abundance to your life.

So the solution: I am going to ask you to be kind to yourself. As simple as this sounds, you will be amazed at how difficult this can be for some. You are so used to analyzing, judging, criticizing yourself it sometimes feels odd to give yourself a break. Again, you are brought back to the traditional conditioning of the harder it is on you, the more you sacrifice, the more value you have as an individual. It's time to expand and move beyond this old belief system and transition into something that is healthier for you as an individual and as a whole. The ease of your experience is grounded in how easy you are with yourself everyday.

BE IT NOW

"You get there by realizing you are already there"
– Eckhart Tolle

I purposefully left this Law of Attraction skill until the end for a few reasons. "Being it now" is about activating the vibration of what you desire for the future, in this moment. It is about being able to deliberately feel the way you think you would feel when you have the manifestation, in this moment, regardless of the external conditions. Being able to master the concept of Being It Now is ultimately the only skill you need to know because it is bringing together all of the other skills we have covered. When you "Be it Now," you will be living what you want NOW.

Remember that the universe is going to match the vibration that you are putting out. If you have a desire for more money in your life, you determine that having money makes you feel abundant and free, the only thing you need to do is feel abundant and free right now (without the physical evidence of the money). When you can consistently do this, the universe must respond by bringing you physical evidence that match the free and abundant emotions.

The Law of Attraction lines up similar frequencies; therefore, if you are acting as if you already have what you want, the universe will respond with more and more evidence to support your most dominant emotion, it is the Law. If my desire is for greater health, I can choose to feel healthy now, and ignore the parts of my reality that show the way it presently is. I can choose to pay more attention to and notice how good my skin looks or how easily my joints move instead of how I have pain in my shins or how tired I always am. You have the choice of what to focus on and as you master this skill, you will have greater and greater access to your wildest desires.

The reason we use other skills like appreciation and self-love is because often times, individuals have a hard time just jumping from a low vibration of fear of poverty to feeling abundant. These tools act to gradually move you up the emotional scale, feeling better and better until you are feeling the emotion you desire. Moving up the emotional scale is actually where all the fun happens, and truly appreciating this part of the journey is an important key to successful manifesting.

The importance and beauty of the journey to what you want.

The majority of people have the process backwards as they wait until they get a new car to be happy, or they wait until they get the better job to feel successful. As you know, we live in a vibrational world and vibrationally, if we get happy first, that new car or that new job comes a lot easier and quicker to us. This is when you say to me, "Wait, I'm pretty sure if I got a new car it would make me very happy." And you are right, it would, temporarily, and then what would you need next to keep that happy feeling? And then what next? Physical things are so fun

There is nothing you need to do, be, or have to feel the way you want to feel right now.

and awesome to enjoy, but if we spend a lifetime letting external circumstances control our emotional states, it will no doubt be an tiresome journey.

Everything in this life is about the "getting there" part. It is about the journey. You are living and creating your life right now in these moments. Think about that desired feeling you want. If you want to be happy, Be it! If you want to be successful, Be it! If you want to be healthy, Be it!

There is nothing you need to do, be, or have to feel the way you want to feel right now.

You get to choose how you feel in every second. The moment we can empower ourselves with this realization, we truly can have anything we desire. If you want it, you can have it. You are FREE.

CHAPTER 6.

How to Speed Up Your Manifesting Results

A fter working with so many clients on leveraging the Law of Attraction, I have noticed a few common places where most people tend to get stuck. At the end of this chapter you will be able to identify certain areas where you may be running into resistance in your alignment with source, and know how to get back on the easy path.

YOU ARE DOING IT RIGHT

Firstly here, I want you to know that you are never doing Law of Attraction wrong. I hear that a lot among my clients during our first session together, and they want to know what they are doing wrong and how to fix it. You can't ever get off your path. Your path is constantly unfolding and where you are is perfect because it is where you are. The only time that you have any power as creators of your life is right now, in this moment. You are where you are and it is ok, why is it ok? Because it is where you are! That's it. There doesn't need to be any other reason. You cannot change where you are in this moment, so you have the choice to allow it or resist it, make peace with it or fight against it. This choice determines if you are pointed upstream or downstream, and whether you are choosing a life of ease or a life of struggle.

Because I know the possibility of being happy all the time, I used to think I was doing LOA wrong if I wasn't feeling good. Catching myself feeling angry, frustrated or sad, I would punish myself, thinking I was doing it wrong. "I know this stuff, I should know how to make myself feel better right now." Eventually I realized, the fact that I thought I was doing it wrong, was the only thing I was doing wrong! Any thought you have that creates a negative feeling within you, is your guidance system nudging you back towards your best path. If you are one of these people, feeling like you are "doing it wrong," catch yourself right now and consciously choose the perspective that you are doing it right. When you deliberately choose this thought, it takes the pressure off of you, releases resistance and allows the universe to bring you to the next step on your path of least resistance.

YOU DON'T HAVE TO FIGURE IT OUT

Absolutely the most prominent place where people get off track in manifesting is their need to make it happen. I understand you have been trained your whole life that if you want something, you need to make it happen. You have an idea, and you need to make a plan and then take all the outlined action steps or what you want won't happen. Well there is something you want right? And you have probably tried to figure out the plan to make it happen, right? And taken the action steps? How is that working out for you?

The thing is when you are trying to figure something out logically in your head and you are thinking about it a lot, you are actually working against the natural laws that really want to bring you want you want. Think about how you feel when you are trying to figure something out. Does it feel exciting or does it feel stressful? Remember your emotions are your guidance system, and your emotions

> *You as a human are not harnessing your full power when you try to think your way through something.*

are what the universe is responding to. So if you are wanting to meet your dream partner and you find yourself thinking about how you are going to meet people or how you can best impress or should I join an online site, you are trying too much, which to the universe is efforting and resistance.

You as a human are not harnessing your full power when you try to think your way through something.

Your true power is known when you allow yourself to be guided by your emotions, which is Source flowing through you.

Resist the urge to logically figure out the how or the plan, and let yourself be guided to the next step. You have the desire, because you have been conditioned to jump right into action when you have an idea, but I am presenting that you actually wait a little bit, revel in the feeling of the desire and wait for your action steps to be inspired.

I do fully believe that action steps are required to achieve a goal or desire, but action without alignment is a waste of your time. IF you want to leverage the Law of Attraction and create a life of ease for yourself, you must learn to trust that the universe has your back and that everything will fall into place without you having to control every little detail. When you are trying really hard to figure something out or make something work, you are going against the natural current and flow of life and it feels like a struggle. If you would just stop trying, and let your feelings be your guide, the easy path to what you want will unfold in front of you.

WANTING VERSUS HAVING

There is a slight difference in vibrations when you are manifesting something, that I feel many people aren't always aware of and has the potential to slow down their results. When you observe something in your reality, you see a couple holding hands and smiling, a preference forms within you, you want to feel that same happiness, so therefore you now have the desire to have a loving relationship. You are aware of your desire and you say "I want a partner." Well the mere statement of "I want…" activates both the desire AND the lack of the desire. As you acknowledge that you want something, you are at the same time acknowledging that you don't have it right now. So when you are wanting something, you are actually sending mixed signals to the universe, and therefore could potentially slow you down from experiencing your desire.

The most powerful way to manifest, as you have already learned, is to act as if you already have the thing you are wanting. You can do this by identifying the feeling you are after and reveling in that feeling when you do experience it in your present reality. With the example of the relationship, you want the partner so you can feel happy and loved. Begin by separating the feeling from the condition, and then deliberately activate the feeling as often as you can, or when you are aware that you are feeling happy and loved, re-affirm to yourself, I am happy and loved. Frame and feel your desires as if they are happening now and you will send clear signals to the universe for speedy manifesting!

CHAPTER 7.

My Wish For You

—————————

About two months ago Alexa reached out to me because she felt stuck where she was, which was moving through a divorce, a single mother, wanting to manifest a new job and a new relationship. She had read about the Law of Attraction and was doing her best to feel positive when she could, but things weren't really manifesting for her. After about 6 weeks of working together, we got on the phone and she was so excited to tell me all of the amazing things that fell into place for her. Her first comment was, everything is so easy now, I get everything I want and I don't even try.

- Unexpected money in the mail
- Finding a long lost piece of jewelry
- Getting everything she wanted out of the divorce, and to her surprise, both she and her ex parted and continue to remain on friendly terms
- The birthday party she planned for her son running easily and smoothly
- Losing 5lbs without even noticing or trying to do anything
- Getting a promotion in her job and actually enjoying the work more

Most importantly, Alexa feels free. She knows now that she has the power to create anything she wants in her life. And my wish for you is to know your power the same way Alexa does.

This life is not a project and you are not here to get anything done.

You never get it done, because you are a naturally and ever expanding being and you are always going to desire something more. If you could step back and understand that it is not about getting the thing, it is about the journey to getting the thing, you could relax and enjoy the journey. Chill out about trying to get somewhere, be something, get something all the time, and appreciate being in this

This life is not a project and you are not here to get anything done.

moment right now. The non-physical entity Abraham, explains it as if you are leaving from Miami on a cruise vacation, and the captain comes on the speaker and says, "alright folks well now that you have boarded the ship, you can go ahead and disembark because we are going to end up in this same location in a week's time anyway." You want the vacation for the experience and the fun along the way. It is not about getting anywhere, or doing anything, it is about feeling and experiencing everything in this life.

After reading this entire book, the one last thing I want to teach you is that words do not teach. Remember when I talked about different types of learning? Intellectual and experiential. You now have the intellectual knowledge about the Law of Attraction and how you can make it work in your life for you. My wish for you is that you take what you have learned and practice it in your life to gain the experiential knowledge. Only once you have felt the feelings and seen the evidence, will you truly make a palpable vibrational shift in your experience.

The key to mastery in anything is consistency. Leveraging the Law of Attraction is a lifestyle, you are literally re-training your brain and thought patterns. Similar to a diet where you can't change your eating patterns for a few months, lose some weight and go back to eating what you normally did and expect to continue to lose weight. You cannot alter your thought patterns for a couple weeks, see results, then go back to old patterns and expect your life to continue to improve. With more and more practice of tuning into your emotions and following your feel good feelings, your life will continue to become one with more and more ease. And yes you can do this on your own, many have great success stories, but for most of you, your real shift and transformation will come from finding someone to work with that can guide your journey. Once Alexa became aware of her vibrations and learned how to clearly and effectively work with the universe, she released the struggle and stepped into her power as a deliberate creator.

Of all of anything I could ever convince you of in this whole world, it would be that you can have whatever you want. That from wherever you are, you can get to where you want to be, and that 100% of everything is possible. For whatever reason, I hold an unwavering belief in the perfection of our universe and the potential of humanity to experience joy and freedom. This knowing is a deep resonance and understanding at a level that cannot be described with words, which I have recently realized is beautiful in itself. Helen Keller describes our existence completely when she said, "The best and most beautiful things in the world cannot been seen or even touched - they must be felt with the heart."

You are here on this planet to feel. Your emotions are your guidance system and your communication with the divine intelligence we call Source energy, which is available to you in every moment and always guiding you. Your purpose here is to have fun, experience joy and create a life of ease. You came into this life as a creator and you HAVE been creating your entire life, but from this point forward you have the awareness to be the deliberate creator of your life. You get to choose how you experience every single thing on this planet, and your choice will determine how you feel, and how you feel will determine what the Law of Attraction will bring to you. The power you hold is incredible, and I am so beyond excited for you to know your value and for you to truly feel you can be do or have anything you desire. It's time to BE the Champion of your own life. Have so much fun with it!

ACKNOWLEDGEMENTS

I was out for a bike ride yesterday and thinking about the incredible amount of individuals who have touched my life over the years. So many teachers, coaches, friends and family that all believed in who I am, and who I am forever appreciative of. I feel like the luckiest woman in the world because I am free to be me and do what I love, which wouldn't be possible without the unconditional support system I have around me.

Mom, Dad and Adam you are my core, and I thank you for all that you are, I wouldn't be me without all of you. To my close friends who have been instrumental in reminding me that it's okay to live life out in left field, your love and support mean the world – and thank you for always highlighting when "you've been coached!"

Cassie, you are the bomb and an inspiration and I love your energy in my life. I am incredibly appreciative of everyone at Difference Press that I begun this journey with; my coach and agent Angela Lauria for your badass attitude and pure genius'ness, and Cynthia Kane for guiding the words of this book perfectly.

Thank you to the team at Morgan James Publishing for making publishing my book such a dream; David Hancock, the Founder of Morgan James Publishing; Jim Howard, the Branding Expert and Publishing Director; Bethany Marshall, the Assistant Publishing Director; Megan Malone, the Author Relations Manager and Nickcole Watkins, the Senior Marketing Relations Manager.

Lastly to my awesome clients who are the coolest people on the whole planet, it is an honour to be co-creating with you and sharing part of this journey together. Totally humbled and blessed.

ABOUT THE AUTHOR

Ginny Gane is a shiny, fun Law of Attraction expert for people who crave more out of life and are ready to realize their full potential. She was raised with the belief anything is possible and we always have a choice.

Ginny lives her life based on the principles of The Law of Attraction, and inspires you to honour your own values and follow your dreams. Her wish is for individuals to break away from what one is "supposed to do," tap into what one really wants to do, and let it flow easily into one's experience. "I would love everyone to wake up in the morning and feel excited and in love with their life," she says and holds the unwavering belief it can be done! Ginny knows that wherever you are, you can get to where you want to be, and the path can be as easy and as fun as you want.

Through her fun and easy courses, ebooks, and personal coaching, she reminds you of your incredible personal power while making it all feel like having an ice cold beer on a hot day. Ahh. Her rockstar followers and clients have called her "uplifting," "a light," and one woman even said "After a session with Ginny, you'll honestly feel as though you can accomplish anything!" When she's not playing with LOA, or co-hosting the popular podcast Manifest It Now, you can find her indulging in sunshiny outdoor adventures, fun fitness exercise and practicing singing...along to the radio.

THANK YOU

Thanks for reading – I am excited about you learning, applying and most significantly, practicing your Law of Attraction skills so that you can really see and feel a difference in your life.

FREE VIDEO COURSE

As a thank you, please enjoy and deepen your understanding with my LOA Skills video training series, where you'll receive tools for everyday alignment:

- *How to get clear about what you want*
- *The best tool for manifesting*
- *How you know you are on the right path*
- *The #1 mistake most LOA'ers make*

To access, simply go to www.loaskillstraining.com

You CAN Have it All!
With so much Fun Love,
Ginny

Morgan James
Speakers Group

www.TheMorganJamesSpeakersGroup.com

We connect Morgan James published
authors with live and online events
and audiences whom will benefit
from their expertise.

Morgan James makes all of our titles available
through the Library for All Charity Organization.

www.LibraryForAll.org

CPSIA information can be obtained
at www.ICGtesting.com
Printed in the USA
JSHW041410060422
24682JS00004B/641

9 781683 503859